Fat-Fighting Foods!

Publications International, Ltd.
Favorite Brand Name Recipes at www.fbnr.com

Copyright © 2000 Publications International, Ltd.
All rights reserved. This publication may not be reproduced or quoted in whole or in part by any means whatsoever without written permission from:

Louis Weber, CEO
Publications International, Ltd.
7373 North Cicero Avenue
Lincolnwood, IL 60712

Permission is never granted for commercial purposes.

Contributing Writers: Gayle Alleman, M.S., R.D.; Densie Webb, Ph.D., R.D.; Susan Male Smith, M.A., R.D.

Nutritional Analysis: Linda R. Yoakam, M.S., R.D., L.D.

Pictured on the front cover: Turkey Sausage & Pasta Toss *(page 62).*

Pictured on the back cover *(clockwise from top):* Tuscan Chicken with White Beans *(page 16),* Spinach and Tomato Tofu Toss *(page 86)* and Maple-Glazed Carrots & Shallots *(page 36).*

ISBN: 0-7853-4751-8

Manufactured in U.S.A.

8 7 6 5 4 3 2 1

Microwave Cooking: Microwave ovens vary in wattage. Use the cooking times as guidelines and check for doneness before adding more time.

Preparation/Cooking Times: Preparation times are based on the approximate amount of time required to assemble the recipe before cooking, baking, chilling or serving. These times include preparation steps such as measuring, chopping and mixing. The fact that some preparations and cooking can be done simultaneously is taken into account. Preparation of optional ingredients and serving suggestions is not included.

Nutritional Analysis: Nutritional information is given for the recipes in this publication. Each analysis is based on the food items in the ingredient list, except ingredients labeled as "optional" or "for garnish." When more than one ingredient choice is listed, the first ingredient is used for analysis. If a range for the amount of an ingredient is given, the nutritional analysis is based on the lowest amount. Foods offered as "serve with" suggestions are not included in the analysis unless otherwise stated.

Note: Neither Publications International, Ltd. nor the authors, editors, or publisher take responsibility for any possible consequences from any treatment, procedure, exercise, dietary modification, action, or application of medication or preparation by any person reading or following the information in this publication. The publication of this book does not constitute the practice of medicine, and this book does not attempt to replace your physician or your pharmacist. Before undertaking any course of treatment, the authors, editors and publisher advise the reader to check with a physician or other health care provider.

Contents

Eating Right

Getting Started

By choosing this publication, you must be ready to fight fat and start eating right. Congratulations! That decision will mean a healthier you, and we will help you get there. By dropping any extra pounds and keeping them off, you'll not only feel better and more energized, you'll also lower your risk of health problems such as heart disease, diabetes and certain cancers. And the best part is, the foods you'll be eating are delicious and filling.

In search for the "perfect" diet, there are many choices. The most successful ones are not diets at all, but actually new ways of eating that become a part of your normal lifestyle. You can lose weight easily—almost magically—when you enjoy foods that promote weight loss by their very nature: foods that are low in calories and fat, rich in fiber and nutrients. This publication will show you how to use those foods to make tasty and satisfying meals.

Don't be fooled by diet schemes that make unrealistic demands such as drinking a liquid diet, focusing on one food group, fasting or starving yourself, or requiring unbalanced meal plans. The best plan for achieving a healthy weight and maintaining it is to gradually change the foods you eat. The fat-fighting foods found here are not gimmicks—they're chockful of satisfying complex carbohydrates, brimming with fiber to give you a feeling of fullness, and rich in nutrients to keep you naturally healthy so your body doesn't crave more food than it needs.

Compared to the standard American diet, the eating plan you are about to embark on is much healthier. It encourages you to eat a variety of complex carbohydrates such as fruits, vegetables, legumes and whole grains with a few dairy and protein foods to keep your body in tip-top shape.

Benefits of Carbohydrates

Complex carbohydrates help to jump-start your metabolism. They are naturally low in calories and rich in fiber, which is especially helpful when you're trying to lose weight. (Fiber helps you feel full, so you don't overeat.) Carbohydrates and protein each contain only four calories per gram, whereas fat contains nine calories per gram. The following chart shows the amount of calories found in a typical serving, versus the amount of calories in a processed form of that food.

Fruit (1 piece) **60 calories**	Fruit pie (1 piece) **300 calories**
Vegetables (½ cup raw) **25 calories**	Potato chips (20) **215 calories**
Bread (1 slice) **80 calories**	Glazed doughnut **242 calories**
Legumes (½ cup) **115 calories**	Ground beef patty **250 calories**

Another reason that eating carbohydrates is encouraged is because the body processes them differently from fat. Fat is broken down, absorbed and stored by the body without much effort, while carbohydrates and protein are more difficult for the body to break down, absorb, process, store and use. It's a much more complicated chemical process to get energy out of carbohydrates and protein than it is to get energy from fat. Thus a diet that is high in complex carbohydrates, low in fat and accompanied by some protein can help you shed unwanted pounds.

The Fiber Factor

It is recommended that everyone eat 20 to 35 grams of fiber each day. Studies repeatedly show that people who eat more fiber, especially the insoluble type, have a lower incidence of colon cancer, and eating more soluble fiber has been shown to lower blood cholesterol. Both kinds of fiber slow the rate at which your stomach empties, as they take a while to work their way through your digestive system. They also enable the sugars in your meal to be absorbed slowly, so you'll feel full a little longer.

Insoluble fiber can be likened to a sponge. When you eat fiber and then add water, it swells and gets soft, just like a sponge. The increased bulk pushes on your intestines, creating the rhythmic movement needed to evacuate. Foods rich in insoluble fiber include bran cereals, brown rice, corn and popcorn, fruits (especially apples, berries and pears), whole grains and vegetables (especially asparagus, kale, peas, potatoes and spinach).

Soluble fiber dissolves in water and forms a gel-like substance which captures bile acids and cholesterol in its wake. Foods rich in soluble fiber include barley, dried beans and peas, fruits (especially apples, figs, oranges, plums and rhubarb), lentils, oats and vegetables (especially broccoli, cabbage, okra and potatoes).

As you change your eating habits and gradually add more fiber-rich complex carbohydrates to your diet, it's absolutely essential that you also begin to drink more water. Without enough fluid, the extra fiber will backfire on you and make you gassy and constipated.

Fighting Fat

Besides filling up on complex carbohydrates, it's important to make low-fat choices. Keep in mind that you do need some fat each day, and not all fats are bad. In fact, the body has to have dietary fat to provide you with the essential fatty acids that cannot be made inside the body. Fat in the diet is also the only way we get the essential fat soluble vitamins A, E and K.

The minimum amount of fat recommended in the diet is 10 to 15 percent of calories. Try to stick to monounsaturated fats, which are predominant in olive and canola oils. Saturated fats, found in animal foods such as meat and dairy products as well as vegetable oils such as coconut and palm kernel oils, should be avoided as much as possible—they should make up no more than a third of the total fats you eat. Other types of fats, such as polyunsaturated (found in most vegetable oils) and hydrogenated (found in most processed and packaged products) should also be used sparingly.

Activity: The Final Ingredient

You've heard it before. You know it's true. If your goal is to lose weight, it's important to do aerobic exercise (to burn fat) as well as strength-training exercises (to build and tone muscles). But now there are more reasons than ever to get moving! Whenever you're active, you're building muscle tissue, and the more muscle you have, the higher your metabolic rate will be. Also, your metabolic rate stays elevated for several hours after physical activity. This metabolic rate—the rate at which you burn calories while at rest—is one of the biggest burners of calories all day long. So if you can pump it up to be burning more calories even when you're not active, you'll shed pounds more easily.

Get Going!

Fighting the fat in your diet and on your body requires an overhaul of your lifestyle, from the choices you make in the supermarket, to how you prepare your meals and how you eat them, to the amount of activity you get each day. Now that you know why fighting fat is so important, it's time to cover those foods we feel fight fat the best. The 26 foods that follow are all low in fat, of course, but they're more than that: they're also high in fiber and rich in nutrients, as you can see in the nutritional analysis of each recipe. You can't go wrong if you eat a wide variety of the choices presented and if you do so in moderation. Eat simply, stay active and enjoy!

Asparagus

Citrus Asparagus

ORANGE SAUCE

- **2 teaspoons reduced-fat margarine**
- **1 clove garlic, minced**
- **Juice of 1 large orange (about ⅓ cup)**
- **1¼ teaspoons balsamic vinegar**
- **¼ teaspoon Dijon mustard**
- **½ teaspoon grated orange peel**
- **Salt (optional)**

ASPARAGUS

- **Olive oil flavored nonstick cooking spray**
- **1 small onion, diced**
- **1 pound fresh asparagus, lower half of stalks peeled***
- **⅔ cup diced red bell pepper**
- **½ cup water**

**If using pencil-thin asparagus, do not peel. Reduce cooking time to 4 to 5 minutes.*

1. For Orange Sauce, heat margarine in small saucepan over medium heat. Add garlic; cook and stir 2 minutes or until soft. Stir in orange juice; bring to a boil. Add vinegar and mustard; reduce heat and simmer 2 minutes. Remove from heat and add orange peel. Season to taste with salt, if desired. Reserve and keep warm.

2. For asparagus, spray medium saucepan with cooking spray; heat over medium-high heat. Add onion; cook and stir 2 minutes. Add asparagus, bell pepper and water. Reduce heat to medium-low. Cover and simmer 7 minutes or until asparagus is crisp-tender. Remove vegetables with slotted spoon to serving dish; serve with reserved Orange Sauce.

Makes 4 servings

Nutrients per Serving

Calories: 58, Calories from Fat: 19%, Total Fat: 1 g, Saturated Fat: <1 g, Protein: 3 g, Carbohydrate: 10 g, Cholesterol: <1 mg, Sodium: 37 mg, Fiber: 2 g

• a very low-calorie food (4 calories per spear) with great flavor

• abundant in major antioxidants beta-carotene and vitamin C, thought to help fight against heart disease, cancer and cataracts

Barley

• contains the same cholesterol-fighting soluble fiber that is found in oat bran and dry beans

• also rich in insoluble fiber, which may help keep digestive disorders at bay

• a versatile ingredient, barley can be baked in casseroles, stuffed into vegetables or served in place of rice. It swells and absorbs water when it cooks, making it the perfect thickener for soups and stews.

Dilly Barley and Corn Salad

4 cups cooked pearled barley, cooled
1 cup frozen corn, thawed
1 cup sliced green onions
½ cup chopped red bell pepper
½ cup chopped green bell pepper
1 lime
½ cup balsamic vinegar
3 tablespoons vegetable oil
1½ teaspoons dill weed
½ teaspoon salt

1. Combine barley, corn, green onions and bell peppers in large bowl.

2. To prepare dressing, grate lime peel to measure ½ teaspoon. Squeeze juice from lime to measure 2 tablespoons. Combine peel and juice in small bowl. Add vinegar, oil, dill weed and salt; whisk to blend. Pour dressing over vegetable mixture; toss to coat.

Makes 12 servings

Nutrients per Serving

Calories: 124, Calories from Fat: 26%, Total Fat: 4 g, Saturated Fat: <1 g, Protein: 2 g, Carbohydrate: 22 g, Cholesterol: 0 mg, Sodium: 94 mg, Fiber: 4 g

Baked Spanish Rice and Barley

- ½ cup chopped onion
- ½ cup chopped green bell pepper
- 2 cloves garlic, minced
- 2 teaspoons vegetable oil
- 1 cup coarsely chopped seeded tomatoes
- 1 cup reduced-sodium chicken broth
- ½ cup uncooked white rice
- ½ cup water
- 3 tablespoons quick-cooking barley
- ¼ teaspoon ground black pepper
- ⅛ teaspoon salt

1. Preheat oven to 350°F. Coat 1½-quart casserole with nonstick cooking spray. Cook and stir onion, bell pepper and garlic in oil in medium saucepan over medium heat until vegetables are tender. Stir in tomatoes, chicken broth, rice, water, barley, black pepper and salt. Bring to a boil over high heat.

2. Pour mixture into prepared casserole. Cover; bake 25 to 30 minutes or until rice and barley are tender and liquid is absorbed. Fluff rice mixture with fork. *Makes 4 servings*

Nutrients per Serving

Calories: 167, Calories from Fat: 16%, Total Fat: 3 g, Saturated Fat: <1 g, Protein: 4 g, Carbohydrate: 32 g, Cholesterol: 0 mg, Sodium: 83 mg, Fiber: 3 g

Vegetable-Barley Pilaf

- ¾ cup chopped onion
- ¾ cup chopped celery
- ¾ cup sliced fresh mushrooms
- 1 cup water
- ¾ cup sliced yellow summer squash
- ½ cup quick-cooking barley
- ½ cup sliced carrots
- ¼ cup chopped fresh parsley
- 2 teaspoons chopped fresh basil *or* ½ teaspoon dried basil leaves, crushed
- ½ teaspoon chicken bouillon granules
- ⅛ teaspoon pepper

Coat large skillet with nonstick cooking spray. Add onion, celery and mushrooms; cook and stir over medium heat until vegetables are tender.

Stir in water, squash, barley, carrots, parsley, basil, bouillon granules and pepper. Bring to a boil over high heat. Reduce heat to medium-low. Cover and simmer 10 to 12 minutes or until barley is tender. *Makes 4 servings*

Nutrients per Serving

Calories: 111, Calories from Fat: 10%, Total Fat: 1 g, Saturated Fat: <1 g, Protein: 4 g, Carbohydrate: 22 g, Cholesterol: 0 mg, Sodium: 147 mg, Fiber: 5 g

Baked Spanish Rice and Barley

Beans

Tuscan Chicken with White Beans

1 large fresh fennel bulb (about ¾ pound)
1 teaspoon olive oil
8 ounces skinless boneless chicken thighs, cut into ¾-inch pieces
1 teaspoon dried rosemary, crushed
½ teaspoon freshly ground black pepper
1 can (14½ ounces) no-salt-added stewed tomatoes, undrained
1 can (about 14 ounces) reduced-sodium chicken broth
1 can (16 or 19 ounces) cannellini beans, rinsed and drained
Hot pepper sauce (optional)

1. Cut off and reserve ¼ cup chopped feathery fennel tops. Chop bulb into ½-inch pieces. Heat oil in large saucepan over medium heat. Add chopped fennel bulb; cook 5 minutes, stirring occasionally.

2. Sprinkle chicken with rosemary and pepper. Add to saucepan; cook and stir 2 minutes. Add tomatoes and chicken broth; bring to a boil. Cover and simmer 10 minutes. Stir in beans; simmer, uncovered, 15 minutes or until chicken is cooked through and sauce thickens. Season to taste with hot sauce, if desired. Ladle into shallow bowls; top with reserved fennel tops.

Makes 4 servings

Prep Time: 15 minutes
Cook Time: 35 minutes

Nutrients per Serving

Calories: 220, Calories from Fat: 27%, Total Fat: 7 g, Saturated Fat: 2 g, Protein: 16 g, Carbohydrate: 24 g, Cholesterol: 34 mg, Sodium: 321 mg

• high in soluble fiber, which lowers blood levels of damaging LDL cholesterol

• also provide substantial insoluble fiber, which helps combat constipation, colon cancer and other conditions afflicting your digestive tract

Polenta with Black Bean Salsa

- Olive oil flavored nonstick cooking spray
- 3 cups water
- 2 teaspoons chicken flavor bouillon granules
- ¾ cup uncooked polenta or stone ground cornmeal
- 1 cup rinsed drained canned black beans
- ¾ cup chunky salsa
- ⅔ cup frozen whole kernel corn, thawed
- ⅓ cup minced fresh cilantro
- 4 teaspoons olive oil
- 6 tablespoons nonfat sour cream

1. Spray 9-inch square pan with cooking spray; set aside.

2. Combine water and bouillon granules in large saucepan; bring to a boil over high heat. Gradually add polenta, stirring constantly with wire whisk. Reduce heat to medium-low. Simmer 10 to 15 minutes or until polenta is thickened and pulls away from side of pan, stirring constantly with wooden spoon. Spread polenta evenly into prepared pan. Cover with plastic wrap; refrigerate 1 to 2 hours or until polenta is firm.

3. Combine beans, salsa, corn and cilantro in medium bowl. Cover with plastic wrap; refrigerate 1 hour. Bring to room temperature before serving.

4. Cut polenta into 6 rectangles; cut each rectangle diagonally to form 2 triangles. Brush both sides of triangles with oil. Spray large nonstick skillet with cooking spray; heat over medium-high heat until hot. Cook triangles, 4 at a time, 6 to 8 minutes or until browned, turning once. Place 2 polenta triangles on each serving plate; top each serving evenly with black bean salsa and sour cream. Garnish as desired.

Makes 6 servings

Nutrients per Serving

Calories: 136, Calories from Fat: 24%, Total Fat: 4 g, Saturated Fat: <1 g, Protein: 6 g, Carbohydrate: 23 g, Cholesterol: 1 mg, Sodium: 639 mg, Fiber: 5 g

Beans are a bonanza of folic acid, copper, iron and magnesium—four nutrients we don't get enough of.

Polenta with Black Bean Salsa

Bran Cereals

Bran and Honey Rye Breadsticks

1 package (¼ ounce) active dry yeast
1 teaspoon sugar
1½ cups warm water (110°F)
3¾ cups all-purpose flour, divided
1 tablespoon honey
1 tablespoon vegetable oil
½ teaspoon salt
1 cup rye flour
½ cup whole bran cereal
Skim milk

1. Dissolve yeast and sugar in warm water in large bowl. Let stand 10 minutes. Add 1 cup all-purpose flour, honey, oil and salt. Beat with electric mixer at medium speed 3 minutes. Stir in rye flour, bran cereal and additional 2 cups all-purpose flour or enough to make moderately stiff dough.

2. Knead dough on lightly floured surface 10 minutes or until smooth and elastic, adding remaining ¾ cup all-purpose flour as necessary to prevent sticking. Place in greased bowl; turn over to grease surface. Cover with damp cloth; let rise in warm place 40 to 45 minutes or until doubled in bulk.

3. Spray 2 baking sheets with nonstick cooking spray. Punch dough down. Divide into 24 equal pieces on lightly floured surface. Roll each piece into an 8-inch rope. Place on prepared baking sheets. Cover with damp cloth; let rise in warm place 30 to 35 minutes or until doubled in bulk.

4. Preheat oven to 375°F. Brush breadsticks with milk. Bake 18 to 20 minutes or until breadsticks are golden brown. Remove from baking sheets. Cool on wire racks.

Makes 24 breadsticks

Nutrients per Serving (2 breadsticks)

Calories: 198, Calories from Fat: 8%, Total Fat: 2 g, Saturated Fat: <1 g, Protein: 5 g, Carbohydrate: 40 g, Cholesterol: 0 mg, Sodium: 109 mg, Fiber: 3 g

• pack more insoluble fiber into one serving than any other food

• help fill you up—insoluble fiber has an amazing capacity to absorb water and expand, and this bulk fools your stomach into thinking you've eaten a lot

Berry Bran Muffins

- **2 cups 100% bran cereal**
- **1¼ cups nonfat milk**
- **½ cup brown sugar, divided**
- **1 egg, slightly beaten**
- **¼ cup vegetable oil**
- **1 teaspoon vanilla**
- **1¼ cups all-purpose flour**
- **1 tablespoon baking powder**
- **¼ teaspoon salt**
- **1 cup blueberries, fresh or frozen (partially thaw if frozen)**

Preheat oven to 350°F. Spray 12-cup muffin pan with nonstick cooking spray.

Mix cereal and milk in medium bowl. Let stand 5 minutes to soften. Reserve 1 tablespoon sugar for topping. Add remaining sugar, egg, oil and vanilla to cereal mixture. Beat well. Combine flour, baking powder and salt in large bowl. Stir in cereal mixture until dry ingredients are just moistened. Gently fold in berries.

Fill muffin cups almost to top. Sprinkle with reserved sugar. Bake 20 to 25 minutes (25 to 30 if using frozen berries) or until toothpick inserted in center comes out clean. Serve warm.

Makes 12 servings

Nutrients per Serving

Calories: 172, Calories from Fat: 27%, Total Fat: 5 g, Saturated Fat: 1 g, Protein: 4 g, Carbohydrate: 29 g, Cholesterol: 18 mg, Sodium: 287 mg, Fiber: 4 g

Bran is not just for breakfast anymore! Try sprinkling bran cereal on yogurt, salads or cut-up fruit, or use it to coat fish or top a casserole.

Berry Bran Muffins

Broccoli

• has more nutrients than most vegetables with very few calories

• a rich source of fiber—half soluble and half insoluble, so you can meet your daily needs for both types

• also a good source of vitamin C, vitamin A, folic acid and calcium

• as a cruciferous vegetable (part of the cabbage family), broccoli contains two important phytochemicals that are thought to be linked with lower rates of cancer

Italian Broccoli with Tomatoes

4 cups broccoli florets
½ cup water
½ teaspoon Italian seasoning, crushed
½ teaspoon dried parsley flakes
¼ teaspoon salt (optional)
⅛ teaspoon pepper
2 medium tomatoes, cut into wedges
½ cup shredded mozzarella cheese

Microwave Directions: Place broccoli and water in 2-quart microwavable casserole; cover. Microwave at HIGH (100% power) 5 to 8 minutes or until crisp-tender. Drain. Stir in Italian seasoning, parsley, salt, pepper and tomatoes. Microwave, uncovered, at HIGH 2 to 4 minutes or until tomatoes are hot. Sprinkle with cheese. Microwave 1 minute or until cheese melts. *Makes 6 servings*

Nutrients per Serving

Calories: 50, Calories from Fat: 30%, Total Fat: 2 g, Saturated Fat: 1 g, Protein: 4 g, Carbohydrate: 5 g, Cholesterol: 5 mg, Sodium: 64 mg, Fiber: 2 g

Farmstand Frittata

Nonstick cooking spray
½ cup chopped onion
1 medium red bell pepper, seeded and cut into thin strips
1 cup broccoli florets, blanched and drained
1 cup cooked, quartered, unpeeled red-skinned potatoes
6 egg whites
1 cup cholesterol-free egg substitute
1 tablespoon chopped fresh parsley
½ teaspoon salt
¼ teaspoon ground black pepper
½ cup (2 ounces) shredded reduced-fat Cheddar cheese

1. Spray large nonstick ovenproof skillet with cooking spray; heat over medium heat until hot. Add onion and bell pepper; cook and stir 3 minutes or until crisp-tender.

2. Add broccoli and potatoes; cook and stir 1 to 2 minutes or until heated through.

3. Whisk together egg whites, egg substitute, parsley, salt and black pepper in medium bowl.

4. Spread vegetables into even layer in skillet. Pour egg white mixture over vegetables; cover and cook over medium heat 10 to 12 minutes or until egg mixture is set.

5. Meanwhile, preheat broiler. Top frittata with cheese. Broil 4 inches from heat 1 minute or until cheese is bubbly and golden brown. Cut into wedges.

Makes 4 servings

Nutrients per Serving

Calories: 179, Calories from Fat: 14%, Total Fat: 3 g, Saturated Fat: 2 g, Protein: 18 g, Carbohydrate: 22 g, Cholesterol: 10 mg, Sodium: 574 mg, Fiber: 3 g

Farmstand Frittata

Bulgur

- rich in insoluble fiber that helps to quickly rid the digestive system of waste and keep it healthy
- inexpensive source of low-fat protein
- a minimally processed food, so it remains high in protein and minerals
- a versatile ingredient, bulgur can be soaked to use in cold salads or used like rice in other recipes

Far East Tabbouleh

¾ cup uncooked bulgur
1¾ cups boiling water
2 tablespoons reduced-sodium teriyaki sauce
2 tablespoons lemon juice
1 tablespoon olive oil
¾ cup diced seeded cucumber
¾ cup diced seeded tomato
½ cup thinly sliced green onions
½ cup minced fresh cilantro or parsley
1 tablespoon minced fresh ginger
1 clove garlic, minced

1. Combine bulgur and water in small bowl. Cover; let stand 45 minutes or until bulgur is puffed, stirring occasionally. Drain and discard liquid.

2. Combine bulgur, teriyaki sauce, lemon juice and oil in large bowl. Stir in cucumber, tomato, onions, cilantro, ginger and garlic until well blended. Cover; refrigerate 4 hours, stirring occasionally. *Makes 4 servings*

Nutrients per Serving

Calories: 73, Calories from Fat: 23%, Total Fat: 2 g, Saturated Fat: <1 g, Protein: 2 g, Carbohydrate: 13 g, Cholesterol: 0 mg, Sodium: 156 mg, Fiber: 3 g

Bulgur Pilaf with Tomato and Zucchini

- 1 cup uncooked bulgur
- 1 tablespoon olive oil
- ¾ cup chopped onion
- 2 cloves garlic, minced
- ½ pound zucchini, thinly sliced
- 1 can (14½ ounces) no-salt-added tomatoes, drained, coarsely chopped
- 1 cup fat-free, reduced-sodium chicken broth
- 1 teaspoon dried basil leaves
- ⅛ teaspoon pepper

Rinse bulgur in colander under cold water. Drain well. Heat oil in large saucepan over medium heat. Add onion and garlic; cook and stir 3 minutes. Stir in zucchini and tomatoes; reduce heat to medium-low. Cook, covered, 15 minutes, or until zucchini is almost tender, stirring occasionally.

Stir in broth, bulgur, basil and pepper. Bring to boil over high heat. Reduce heat to low. Cook, covered, 15 minutes or until liquid is almost completely absorbed, stirring occasionally. Remove from heat; let stand, covered, 10 minutes. *Makes 8 servings*

Nutrients per Serving

Calories: 98, Calories from Fat: 19%, Total Fat: 2 g, Saturated Fat: <1 g, Protein: 3 g, Carbohydrate: 18 g, Cholesterol: 0 mg, Sodium: 92 mg, Fiber: 5 g

Mediterranean Chicken Salad

- 1 box (5¼ ounces) quick-cooking bulgur wheat
- ¾ pound chicken tenders
- 1 tablespoon olive oil
- 1 cup chopped tomato
- 1 cup chopped fresh parsley
- 2 green onions, sliced
- 2 tablespoons lemon juice
- Salt and black pepper

1. Prepare bulgur according to package directions; set aside.

2. While bulgur is cooking, cut chicken tenders into 1-inch pieces. Heat olive oil in medium skillet. Add chicken; cook and stir until no longer pink in center. Remove from heat; cool slightly.

3. Combine cooked bulgur, chicken, tomato, parsley, green onions and lemon juice in large bowl; toss gently to blend. Season with salt and pepper to taste. *Makes 4 servings*

Prep and Cook Time: 20 minutes

Nutrients per Serving

Calories: 277, Calories from Fat: 19%, Total Fat: 6 g, Protein: 24 g, Carbohydrate: 32 g, Cholesterol: 52 mg, Sodium: 64 mg, Fiber: 9 g

Mediterranean Chicken Salad

Cabbage

- very low in calories and fat (among the lowest numbers of any vegetable)
- green cabbage provides a good amount of fiber and vitamin C
- some types of cabbage, such as bok choy (Chinese cabbage), are an important source of calcium and beta-carotene

Jalapeño Cole Slaw

6 cups preshredded cabbage or coleslaw mix
2 tomatoes, seeded and chopped
6 green onions, coarsely chopped
2 jalapeño peppers, finely chopped
¼ cup cider vinegar
3 tablespoons honey
1 teaspoon salt

1. Combine cabbage, tomatoes, green onions, jalapeños, vinegar, honey and salt in serving bowl; mix well. Cover and chill at least 2 hours before serving.

2. Stir well immediately before serving.

Makes 4 servings

Note: For a milder cole slaw, discard the seeds and veins when chopping the jalapeños, as this is where much of the heat of the peppers is stored.

Nutrients per Serving

Calories: 94, Calories from Fat: 4%, Total Fat: <1 g, Saturated Fat: <1 g, Protein: 2 g, Carbohydrate: 24 g, Cholesterol: 0 mg, Sodium: 608 mg, Fiber: 3 g

Chinese Cabbage Salad

- 6 tablespoons cider vinegar
- 3 tablespoons sugar
- 1 tablespoon dark sesame oil
- 1 teaspoon minced fresh ginger
- 1 large crisp red apple, diced
- 1 medium (1 to 1¼ pounds) head green cabbage *or* 1 bag (16 ounces) prepackaged shredded coleslaw mix
- 2 green onions, thinly sliced
- ⅓ cup golden raisins
- 2 tablespoons chopped fresh cilantro
- 1 tablespoon toasted sesame seeds

1. Combine vinegar, sugar, oil and ginger in large bowl; stir until sugar dissolves. Stir in apple.

2. Add cabbage, onions, raisins, cilantro and sesame seeds; gently stir until well combined.

Makes 6 servings

Note: Store cabbage tightly wrapped in a plastic bag in the refrigerator for up to two weeks. A 1-pound cabbage will yield about 4 cups shredded cabbage.

Nutrients per Serving

Calories: 115, Calories from Fat: 23%, Total Fat: 3 g, Saturated Fat: <1 g, Protein: 2 g, Carbohydrate: 23 g, Cholesterol: 0 mg, Sodium: 16 mg, Fiber: 3 g

Red Cabbage with Apples

- 1 small head red cabbage, shredded
- 2 large apples, peeled and thinly sliced
- ½ cup sliced onion
- ½ cup unsweetened apple juice
- ¼ cup lemon juice
- 2 tablespoons raisins
- 2 tablespoons brown sugar
- Salt and pepper to taste (optional)

Combine cabbage, apples, onion, apple juice, lemon juice, raisins and brown sugar in large nonstick saucepan. Simmer, covered, 30 minutes. Season with salt and pepper.

Makes 8 servings

Nutrients per Serving

Calories: 68, Calories from Fat: 3%, Total Fat: <1 g, Saturated Fat: <1 g, Protein: 1 g, Carbohydrate: 17 g, Cholesterol: 0 mg, Sodium: 13 mg, Fiber: 2 g

Red Cabbage with Apples

Carrots

- contain an uncommon amount of beta-carotene: a half-cup serving of cooked carrots packs four times the recommended daily allowance of vitamin A in the form of beta-carotene

- very little nutritional value is lost in cooking (unless the carrots are overcooked until mushy)—and the nutrients in lightly cooked carrots are more usable by your body than those in raw carrots

Maple-Glazed Carrots & Shallots

1 package (16 ounces) baby carrots
1 tablespoon margarine or butter
½ cup thinly sliced shallots
2 tablespoons reduced-fat maple-flavored pancake syrup
¼ teaspoon salt
⅛ teaspoon white pepper

1. Place carrots in medium saucepan. Add enough water to cover carrots. Simmer 8 to 10 minutes or until carrots are tender. Drain; set aside.

2. In same saucepan, melt margarine over medium-high heat. Add shallots; cook and stir 3 to 4 minutes or until shallots begin to brown. Add carrots, syrup, salt and pepper. Cook and stir 1 to 2 minutes or until carrots are coated and heated through.

Makes 4 servings

Nutrients per Serving

Calories: 80, Calories from Fat: 31%, Total Fat: 3 g, Saturated Fat: 1 g, Protein: <1 g, Carbohydrate: 14 g, Cholesterol: 0 mg, Sodium: 279 mg, Fiber: 3 g

Polynesian Ginger Carrots

- 1 pound carrots, cut diagonally into ⅛-inch-thick slices
- 1 can (6 ounces) unsweetened pineapple juice
- ½ cup finely chopped onion
- 1½ teaspoons cornstarch
- 1 tablespoon water
- 1 teaspoon reduced-sodium soy sauce
- ½ teaspoon ground ginger
- 2 teaspoons toasted sesame seeds*

**To toast sesame seeds, cook in small nonstick skillet over medium heat 3 minutes or until golden brown, stirring constantly. Remove from skillet; let cool.*

Combine carrots, pineapple juice and onion in medium saucepan. Bring to a boil. Reduce heat to low. Simmer, covered, 10 minutes or until carrots are crisp-tender, stirring once. Blend cornstarch with water until smooth. Stir cornstarch mixture, soy sauce and ginger into saucepan with carrots. Cook and stir over medium heat until sauce boils and thickens. Cook and stir 1 minute more. Sprinkle with sesame seeds. *Makes 4 servings*

Nutrients per Serving

Calories: 92, Calories from Fat: 9%, Total Fat: 1 g, Saturated Fat: <1 g, Protein: 2 g, Carbohydrate: 20 g, Cholesterol: 0 mg, Sodium: 85 mg, Fiber: 4 g

Apple & Carrot Casserole

- 6 large carrots, sliced
- 4 large apples, peeled, halved, cored and sliced
- 5 tablespoons all-purpose flour
- 1 tablespoon packed brown sugar
- ½ teaspoon ground nutmeg
- 1 tablespoon margarine
- ½ cup orange juice
- ½ teaspoon salt (optional)

Preheat oven to 350°F. Cook carrots in large saucepan in boiling water 5 minutes; drain. Layer carrots and apples in large casserole. Combine flour, sugar and nutmeg; sprinkle over top. Dot with margarine; pour orange juice over flour mixture. Bake 30 minutes or until carrots are tender. *Makes 6 servings*

Nutrients per Serving

Calories: 144, Calories from Fat: 15%, Total Fat: 3 g, Saturated Fat: 1 g, Protein: 2 g, Carbohydrate: 31 g, Cholesterol: 0 mg, Sodium: 49 mg, Fiber: 5 g

Apple & Carrot Casserole

Cauliflower

Light Lemon Cauliflower

- **¼ cup chopped fresh parsley, divided**
- **½ teaspoon grated lemon peel**
- **6 cups (about 1½ pounds) cauliflower florets**
- **1 tablespoon reduced-fat margarine**
- **3 cloves garlic, minced**
- **2 tablespoons fresh lemon juice**
- **¼ cup grated Parmesan cheese**

1. Place 1 tablespoon parsley, lemon peel and about 1 inch of water in large saucepan. Place cauliflower in steamer basket and place in saucepan. Bring water to a boil over medium heat. Cover and steam 14 to 16 minutes or until cauliflower is crisp-tender. Remove to large bowl; keep warm. Reserve ½ cup hot liquid.

2. Heat margarine in small saucepan over medium heat. Add garlic; cook and stir 2 to 3 minutes or until soft. Stir in lemon juice and reserved liquid.

3. Spoon lemon sauce over cauliflower. Sprinkle with remaining 3 tablespoons parsley and cheese before serving. Garnish with lemon slices, if desired.

Makes 6 servings

Nutrients per Serving

Calories: 53, Calories from Fat: 33%, Total Fat: 2 g, Saturated Fat: 1 g, Protein: 4 g, Carbohydrate: 6 g, Cholesterol: 3 mg, Sodium: 116 mg, Fiber: 3 g

- one of the best sources of vitamin C after citrus fruits
- high in fiber, folic acid and potassium
- contains phytochemicals called indoles that may stimulate enzymes that block cancer growth

Corn

Mexican Hot Pot

- **1 tablespoon canola oil**
- **1 onion, sliced**
- **3 cloves garlic, minced**
- **2 teaspoons red pepper flakes**
- **2 teaspoons dried oregano leaves, crushed**
- **1 teaspoon ground cumin**
- **1 can (28 ounces) tomatoes, chopped**
- **1 can (15 ounces) chick-peas (garbanzo beans), rinsed and drained**
- **1 can (15 ounces) pinto beans, rinsed and drained**
- **2 cups whole kernel corn, fresh or frozen**
- **1 cup water**
- **6 cups shredded iceberg lettuce**

1. Heat oil in stockpot or Dutch oven over medium-high heat. Add onion and garlic; cook and stir 5 minutes. Add red pepper flakes, oregano and cumin; mix well.

2. Stir in tomatoes, chick-peas, pinto beans, corn and water; bring to a boil over high heat.

3. Reduce heat to medium-low; cover and simmer 15 minutes. Top individual servings with 1 cup shredded lettuce. Serve hot. *Makes 6 servings*

Nutrients per Serving

Calories: 252, Calories from Fat: 16%, Total Fat: 5 g, Saturated Fat: <1 g, Protein: 12 g, Carbohydrate: 46 g, Cholesterol: 0 mg, Sodium: 765 mg, Fiber: 7 g

• a low-fat complex carbohydrate that can curb your appetite for high-fat foods

• high in insoluble fiber, which helps to prevent common digestive ailments

• a surprising source of several vitamins, including folic acid, niacin and vitamin C

Fish & Shellfish

- low in fat (generally 20 percent or less of total calories)
- the oil contained in fish, omega-3 fatty acids, are thought to offer some amazing health benefits, including fighting heart disease and boosting HDL (good) cholesterol
- studies show that eating a few servings of fish each week reduces the chance of a heart attack by one-third to one-half

Broiled Hunan Fish Fillets

3 tablespoons low-sodium soy sauce
1 tablespoon finely chopped green onion
2 teaspoons dark sesame oil
1 clove garlic, minced
1 teaspoon minced fresh ginger
¼ teaspoon red pepper flakes
Nonstick cooking spray
1 pound red snapper, scrod or cod fillets

1. Combine soy sauce, onion, oil, garlic, ginger and red pepper flakes in small bowl.

2. Spray rack of broiler pan with nonstick cooking spray. Place fish on rack; brush with soy sauce mixture.

3. Broil 4 to 5 inches from heat 10 minutes or until fish flakes easily with fork. Serve on lettuce-lined plate, if desired. *Makes 4 servings*

Nutrients per Serving

Calories: 144, Calories from Fat: 24%, Total Fat: 4 g, Saturated Fat: <1 g, Protein: 25 g, Carbohydrate: 1 g, Cholesterol: 42 mg, Sodium: 446 mg, Fiber: <1 g

Broccoli, Scallop and Linguine Toss

- 12 ounces fresh or frozen scallops
- 2 medium onions, cut in half lengthwise and sliced
- 1 cup apple juice
- 2 tablespoons dry white wine
- 2 cloves garlic, minced
- 2 teaspoons dried marjoram leaves
- 1 teaspoon dried basil leaves
- ¼ teaspoon pepper
- 3 cups broccoli flowerets
- ¼ cup water
- 4 teaspoons cornstarch
- 1½ cups chopped seeded tomatoes
- ¼ cup grated Parmesan cheese
- 4 cups cooked linguine

Cut large scallops into 1-inch pieces. Combine onions, apple juice, wine, garlic, marjoram, basil and pepper in large skillet. Bring to a boil over high heat. Add broccoli; return to a boil. Reduce heat to medium-low. Cover and simmer 7 minutes; add scallops. Return to a boil; reduce heat. Cover and simmer 1 to 2 minutes or until scallops are opaque. Remove scallops and vegetables, leaving liquid in skillet.

Combine water and cornstarch in small bowl. Stir into mixture in skillet. Cook and stir over medium heat until mixture boils and thickens. Cook and stir 2 minutes more. Stir in tomatoes and cheese; heat through. Return scallops and vegetables to skillet; heat through. Toss mixture with linguine.

Makes 4 servings

Nutrients per Serving

Calories: 248, Calories from Fat: 13%, Total Fat: 4 g, Saturated Fat: 1 g, Protein: 22 g, Carbohydrate: 33 g, Cholesterol: 33 mg, Sodium: 309 mg, Fiber: 4 g

Scallops cook very quickly (about 1 to 3 minutes); like all other seafood they become tough when overcooked.

Broccoli, Scallop and Linguine Toss

Broiled Tuna and Raspberry Salad

½ cup fat-free ranch salad dressing
¼ cup raspberry vinegar
1½ teaspoons Cajun seasoning
1 thick-sliced tuna steak (about 6 to 8 ounces)
2 cups torn romaine lettuce leaves
1 cup torn mixed baby lettuce leaves
½ cup fresh raspberries

1. Combine salad dressing, vinegar and Cajun seasoning. Pour ¼ cup salad dressing mixture into resealable plastic food storage bag to use as marinade, reserving remaining mixture. Add tuna to marinade. Seal bag; turn to coat tuna. Marinate in the refrigerator 10 minutes, turning once.

2. Preheat broiler. Spray rack of broiler pan with nonstick cooking spray. Place tuna on rack. Broil tuna, 4 inches from heat, 5 minutes. Turn tuna and brush with marinade; discard remaining marinade. Broil 5 minutes more or until tuna flakes in center. Cool 5 minutes. Cut into ¼-inch slices.

3. Toss lettuces together in large bowl; divide evenly between two serving plates. Top with tuna and raspberries; drizzle with reserved salad dressing mixture. *Makes 2 servings*

Prep and Cook Time: 27 minutes

Nutrients per Serving

Calories: 215, Calories from Fat: 22%, Total Fat: 5 g, Saturated Fat: 1 g, Protein: 24 g, Carbohydrate: 18 g, Cholesterol: 35 mg, Sodium: 427 mg, Fiber: 5 g

- cooking greens provide an important source of nondairy calcium, and most are a great source of vitamin A as well
- darker salad greens (the darker the green, the more nutritious it is) contain disease-fighting beta-carotene and many other antioxidants

Lentils

Curried Lentils with Fruit

1½ cups uncooked lentils, rinsed, sorted and drained*
1 Granny Smith apple, cored, peeled and chopped
¼ cup golden raisins
¼ cup lemon nonfat yogurt
1 teaspoon curry powder
1 teaspoon salt

**Packages of dried lentils may contain grit and tiny stones. Therefore, thoroughly rinse lentils, then sort through and discard grit or any unusual looking pieces.*

1. Combine 2 quarts water and lentils in large saucepan; bring to a boil over high heat. Reduce heat to medium-low. Simmer 20 minutes, stirring occasionally.

2. Stir apple and raisins into saucepan; cook 10 minutes or until lentils are tender. Drain lentil mixture; discard liquid.

3. Place lentil mixture in large serving bowl; stir in yogurt, curry powder and salt until well blended. Garnish as desired. *Makes 6 servings*

Tip: Apples brown easily once they are cut. To prevent undesirable browning, sprinkle lemon, apple or grapefruit juice over apple pieces.

Nutrients per Serving

Calories: 160, Calories from Fat: 3%, Total Fat: 1 g, Saturated Fat: <1 g, Protein: 10 g, Carbohydrate: 31 g, Cholesterol: <1 mg, Sodium: 364 mg, Fiber: 6 g

• a great source of low-fat protein—the perfect substitute for fattier cuts of meat

• high fiber content, most of which is the soluble kind that helps lower blood-cholesterol levels

• an important source of iron for vegetarians, lentils protect against anemia

Zesty Lentil Stew

- **1 cup dried lentils**
- **2 cups chopped peeled potatoes**
- **1 can (about 14 ounces) fat-free, reduced-sodium chicken broth**
- **1⅔ cups water**
- **1½ cups chopped seeded tomatoes**
- **1 can (11½ ounces) no-salt-added spicy vegetable juice cocktail**
- **1 cup chopped onion**
- **½ cup chopped carrot**
- **½ cup chopped celery**
- **2 tablespoons chopped fresh basil *or* 2 teaspoons dried basil leaves**
- **2 tablespoons chopped fresh oregano *or* 2 teaspoons dried oregano leaves**
- **1 to 2 tablespoons finely chopped jalapeño pepper***
- **¼ teaspoon salt**

**Jalapeño peppers can sting and irritate the skin; wear rubber gloves when handling peppers and do not touch eyes. Wash your hands after handling peppers.*

Rinse lentils under cold water; drain. Combine lentils, potatoes, broth, water, tomatoes, vegetable juice cocktail, onion, carrot, celery, basil, oregano, jalapeño pepper and salt in 3-quart saucepan.

Bring to a boil over high heat. Reduce heat to medium-low. Cover; simmer 45 to 50 minutes or until lentils are tender, stirring occasionally.

Makes 4 servings

Nutrients per Serving

Calories: 369, Calories from Fat: 3%, Total Fat: 1 g, Saturated Fat: <1 g, Protein: 19 g, Carbohydrate: 72 g, Cholesterol: 0 mg, Sodium: 620 mg, Fiber: 7 g

Unlike dried beans, lentils don't need to be soaked before cooking. But they should be rinsed in a colander before using.

Zesty Lentil Stew

Mushrooms

Spinach and Mushroom Risotto

Olive oil flavored nonstick cooking spray
½ pound mushrooms, sliced
2 teaspoons dried basil leaves
2 teaspoons minced garlic
¼ teaspoon black pepper
1 can (about 14 ounces) fat-free, reduced-sodium chicken broth
1½ cups uncooked arborio rice
1 can (10¾ ounces) reduced-fat, reduced-sodium condensed cream of mushroom soup, undiluted
1⅔ cups water
3 cups packed spinach leaves, chopped
6 tablespoons chopped walnuts, toasted
¼ cup grated Parmesan cheese

1. Spray 3-quart saucepan with cooking spray; heat over high heat. Add mushrooms, basil, garlic and pepper; cook and stir 3 to 4 minutes or until mushrooms are tender.

2. Stir in broth, rice, soup and water; cook and stir until well blended and mixture begins to boil. Reduce heat to low. Cover; simmer gently 12 minutes, stirring twice during cooking or until rice is just tender but still firm to the bite.

3. Stir in spinach; cover and let stand 5 to 7 minutes or until spinach is wilted.

4. Sprinkle with walnuts and cheese before serving.

Makes 8 (1-cup) servings

Nutrients per Serving

Calories: 219, Calories from Fat: 19%, Total Fat: 5 g, Saturated Fat: 1 g, Protein: 8 g, Carbohydrate: 37 g, Cholesterol: 2 mg, Sodium: 250 mg, Fiber: 3 g

• low in fat while lending wonderful flavor to foods

• cooked mushrooms are higher in nutrients than raw mushrooms—cooking removes water, concentrating nutrients and flavor

Oats

Oat Cakes with Fresh Fruit Topping

- 1 pint hulled strawberries, raspberries or blueberries, divided
- ½ cup sugar, divided
- 2 tablespoons cornstarch
- ½ cup water
- 1 teaspoon lemon juice
- ½ cup uncooked oats
- 1 cup whole wheat flour
- 2½ teaspoons baking powder
- 1¼ cups skim milk
- ½ cup plain nonfat yogurt
- Nonstick cooking spray

Place half of strawberries in medium bowl; mash with potato masher. Slice remaining strawberries; set aside. (If using raspberries or blueberries, do not slice.)

Combine ⅓ cup sugar and cornstarch in small saucepan. Stir in water until cornstarch is dissolved. Cook and stir over medium heat until mixture comes to a boil. Add lemon juice and mashed strawberries; return to a boil. Remove from heat; let stand 15 minutes. Stir in sliced strawberries.

Stir oats in heavy skillet over medium heat 3 minutes or until slightly browned. Turn into medium bowl; cool 10 minutes. Stir in flour, baking powder and remaining sugar. Combine milk and yogurt in small bowl; stir into flour mixture just until all ingredients are moistened. (Batter will be lumpy.)

Coat nonstick griddle or heavy skillet with nonstick cooking spray. Heat over medium heat until water droplets sprinkled on griddle bounce off surface. Drop batter by scant ¼ cupfuls onto griddle; spread batter to form 4-inch round cakes. Cook 2 minutes or until bubbles appear on entire top of batter. Turn cakes; cook 2 minutes longer or until browned. Serve warm with fruit sauce.

Makes 6 servings (2 oat cakes and ⅓ cup sauce per serving)

Nutrients per Serving

Calories: 209, Calories from Fat: 5%, Total Fat: 1 g, Saturated Fat: <1 g, Protein: 7 g, Carbohydrate: 45 g, Cholesterol: 1 mg, Sodium: 0 mg, Fiber: 4 g

- an impressive source of fat-fighting soluble fiber, shown to reduce blood-cholesterol levels

- this soluble fiber also slows digestion, which means you feel full longer

Parsnips

Carrot and Parsnip Purée

- **1 pound carrots, peeled**
- **1 pound parsnips, peeled**
- **1 cup chopped onion**
- **1 cup vegetable broth**
- **1 tablespoon margarine**
- **⅛ teaspoon nutmeg**

1. Cut carrots and parsnips crosswise into ½-inch pieces.

2. Combine carrots, parsnips, onions and vegetable broth in medium saucepan. Cover; bring to a boil over high heat. Reduce heat; simmer, covered, 20 to 22 minutes or until vegetables are very tender.

3. Drain vegetables, reserving broth. Combine vegetables, margarine, nutmeg and ¼ cup reserved broth in food processor. Process until smooth. Serve immediately or transfer to microwave-safe casserole and chill up to 24 hours.

4. To reheat, cover and microwave at HIGH 6 to 7 minutes, stirring after 4 minutes of cooking.

Makes 6 servings

Nutrients per Serving

Calories: 129, Calories from Fat: 15%, Total Fat: 2 g, Saturated Fat: <1 g, Protein: 2 g, Carbohydrate: 27 g, Cholesterol: <1 mg, Sodium: 93 mg, Fiber: 4 g

• high in soluble fiber, which helps lower cholesterol and keeps blood sugar on an even keel

• provide an ample amount of potassium and folic acid

Pasta

Pasta Peperonata

- Olive oil flavored nonstick cooking spray
- 4 cups sliced green, red and yellow bell peppers (about 1 large pepper of each color)
- 4 cups sliced onions
- 3 cloves garlic, minced
- 1 teaspoon dried basil leaves
- ½ teaspoon dried marjoram leaves
- Salt and black pepper
- 4 ounces spaghetti or linguini, cooked and kept warm
- 4 teaspoons grated Parmesan cheese

1. Spray large skillet with cooking spray. Heat over medium heat until hot. Add bell peppers, onions, garlic, basil and marjoram; cook, covered, 8 to 10 minutes or until vegetables are wilted. Uncover; cook and stir 20 to 30 minutes or until onions are caramelized and mixture is soft and creamy. Season to taste with salt and black pepper.

2. Spoon pasta onto plates; top with peperonata and cheese.

Makes 6 side-dish servings

Nutrients per Serving

Calories: 176, Calories from Fat: 7%, Total Fat: 1 g, Saturated Fat: <1 g, Protein: 6 g, Carbohydrate: 37 g, Cholesterol: 1 mg, Sodium: 31 mg, Fiber: 6 g

• the ideal carbo-loading food for athletes, packing in complex carbohydrates with just the right amount of protein and essentially no fat

• whole wheat pasta is particularly rich in minerals and fiber

• a low-calorie complex carbohydrate (4 calories per gram) that is digested slowly

Turkey Sausage & Pasta Toss

- 8 ounces uncooked penne or gemelli pasta
- 1 can (14½ ounces) no-salt-added stewed tomatoes, undrained
- 6 ounces turkey kielbasa or smoked turkey sausage
- 2 cups fresh asparagus pieces (1 inch) or broccoli florets
- 2 tablespoons prepared reduced-fat pesto sauce
- 2 tablespoons grated Parmesan cheese

1. Cook pasta according to package directions, omitting salt.

2. Meanwhile, heat tomatoes in medium saucepan. Cut sausage crosswise into ¼-inch slices; add to tomatoes. Stir in asparagus and pesto; cover and simmer about 6 minutes or until asparagus is crisp-tender.

3. Drain pasta; toss with tomato mixture and sprinkle with cheese.

Makes 4 servings

Prep & Cook Time: 25 minutes

Nutrients per Serving

Calories: 342, Calories from Fat: 18%, Total Fat: 7 g, Saturated Fat: 2 g, Protein: 18 g, Carbohydrate: 53 g, Cholesterol: 30 mg, Sodium: 483 mg, Fiber: 5 g

Orzo with Spinach and Red Pepper

- 4 ounces uncooked orzo
- 1 teaspoon olive oil
- 1 medium red bell pepper, diced
- 3 cloves garlic, minced
- 1 package (10 ounces) frozen chopped spinach, thawed and squeezed dry
- ¼ cup grated Parmesan cheese
- ½ teaspoon minced fresh oregano or basil (optional)
- ¼ teaspoon lemon pepper

1. Prepare orzo according to package directions; drain well and set aside.

2. Spray large nonstick skillet with nonstick cooking spray. Heat skillet over medium-high heat until hot and add oil, tilting skillet to coat bottom. Add bell pepper and garlic; cook and stir 2 to 3 minutes or until bell pepper is crisp-tender. Add orzo and spinach; stir until evenly mixed and heated through. Remove from heat and stir in Parmesan cheese, oregano, if desired, and lemon pepper. Garnish as desired.

Makes 6 servings

Nutrients per Serving

Calories: 116, Calories from Fat: 19%, Total Fat: 3 g, Saturated Fat: 1 g, Protein: 6 g, Carbohydrate: 19 g, Cholesterol: 3 mg, Sodium: 152 mg, Fiber: 2 g

Orzo with Spinach and Red Pepper

Peas

Double Pea Soup

1 tablespoon vegetable oil
1 large white onion, finely chopped
3 cloves garlic, finely chopped
2 cups water
2 cups dried split peas
1 bay leaf
1 teaspoon ground mustard
1½ cups frozen green peas
1 teaspoon salt
¼ teaspoon ground black pepper
Nonfat sour cream (optional)

1. Heat oil in large saucepan or Dutch oven over medium-high heat until hot. Add onion; cook 5 minutes or until onion is tender, stirring occasionally. Add garlic; cook and stir 2 minutes.

2. Stir water, split peas, bay leaf and mustard into saucepan. Bring to a boil over high heat. Cover; reduce heat to medium-low. Simmer 45 minutes or until split peas are tender, stirring occasionally.

3. Stir green peas, salt and pepper into saucepan; cover. Cook 10 minutes or until green peas are tender. Remove bay leaf; discard. Blend using hand-held blender until smooth or process small batches in blender or food processor until smooth.

4. Top each serving with sour cream before serving. Garnish as desired.

Makes 6 servings

Note: If a smoky flavor is desired, a chipotle chili can be added during the last 5 minutes of cooking.

Nutrients per Serving

Calories: 290, Calories from Fat: 10%, Total Fat: 3 g, Saturated Fat: <1 g, Protein: 19 g, Carbohydrate: 48 g, Cholesterol: 0 mg, Sodium: 401 mg, Fiber: 5 g

• twice the protein of most vegetables
• outstanding source of vitamins A, B and C
• chockful of nutrients, including iron (it's difficult to find other nonanimal foods with as much)

Potatoes

- very low in fat and high in fiber (half soluble and half insoluble, so potatoes will help lower cholesterol and keep you full longer)
- rich source of vitamin C
- high in potassium, as well as iron and copper
- with the exception of vitamin A, potatoes contain just about every nutrient

Roast Cajun Potatoes

1 pound baking potatoes
2 tablespoons finely chopped parsley
2 teaspoons canola oil
½ teaspoon garlic powder
½ teaspoon onion powder
½ teaspoon ground red pepper
½ teaspoon dried thyme leaves
¼ teaspoon black pepper

1. Preheat oven to 400°F. Peel potatoes; cut each potato lengthwise into 8 wedges. Place on ungreased jelly-roll pan or cookie sheet.

2. Toss potatoes with parsley, oil, garlic powder, onion powder, red pepper, thyme and black pepper until evenly coated.

3. Bake 50 minutes, turning wedges halfway through cooking time. Serve immediately. *Makes 4 servings*

Nutrients per Serving

Calories: 120, Calories from Fat: 18%, Total Fat: 2 g, Saturated Fat: <1 g, Protein: 2 g, Carbohydrate: 23 g, Cholesterol: 0 mg, Sodium: 7 mg, Fiber: 2 g

Potatoes au Gratin

- **1 pound baking potatoes**
- **4 teaspoons reduced-calorie margarine**
- **4 teaspoons all-purpose flour**
- **1¼ cups fat-free (skim) milk**
- **¼ teaspoon ground nutmeg**
- **¼ teaspoon paprika**
- **Pinch ground white pepper**
- **½ cup thinly sliced red onion, divided**
- **⅓ cup whole wheat bread crumbs**
- **1 tablespoon finely chopped red onion**
- **1 tablespoon grated Parmesan cheese**

1. Spray 4- or 6-cup casserole with nonstick cooking spray; set aside.

2. Place potatoes in large saucepan; add water to cover. Bring to a boil over high heat. Boil 12 minutes or until potatoes are tender. Drain; let potatoes stand 10 minutes or until cool enough to handle.

3. Melt margarine in small saucepan over medium heat. Add flour. Cook and stir 3 minutes or until small clumps form. Gradually whisk in milk. Cook 8 minutes or until sauce thickens, stirring constantly. Remove saucepan from heat. Stir in nutmeg, paprika and pepper.

4. Preheat oven to 350°F. Cut potatoes into thin slices. Arrange half of potato slices in prepared casserole. Sprinkle with half of onion slices. Repeat layers. Spoon sauce over potato mixture. Combine bread crumbs, finely chopped red onion and cheese in small bowl. Sprinkle mixture evenly over sauce.

5. Bake 20 minutes. Let stand 5 minutes before serving. Garnish as desired. *Makes 4 servings*

Nutrients per Serving

Calories: 178, Calories from Fat: 14%, Total Fat: 3 g, Saturated Fat: 1 g, Protein: 6 g, Carbohydrate: 33 g, Cholesterol: 2 mg, Sodium: 144 mg, Fiber: 2 g

Potatoes au Gratin

Rice

Vegetable Paella

- ½ cup chopped onion
- 1 clove garlic, minced
- Olive oil flavored nonstick cooking spray
- 1 can (about 14 ounces) fat-free, reduced-sodium chicken or vegetable broth
- 1 cup uncooked rice
- 1 cup chopped plum tomatoes
- ¼ cup water
- ½ teaspoon dried oregano
- ½ teaspoon chili powder
- ⅛ teaspoon turmeric
- ⅛ teaspoon salt
- Black pepper
- 1 red bell pepper, cut into short strips
- 1 jar (6 ounces) marinated artichoke hearts, drained and quartered
- ½ cup frozen peas
- ⅛ teaspoon hot pepper sauce

1. Place onion and garlic in 2-quart microwavable casserole. Spray lightly with cooking spray. Microwave at HIGH 30 seconds.

2. Add broth, rice, tomatoes, water, oregano, chili powder, turmeric, salt and black pepper. Cover with vented plastic wrap. Microwave at HIGH 5 minutes. Stir in bell pepper, artichokes, peas and hot sauce. Microwave at MEDIUM (50%) 15 to 18 minutes or until broth is absorbed and rice is tender. *Makes 4 servings*

Note: If plum tomatoes are unavailable, substitute 1 can (14½ ounces) undrained diced tomatoes. Omit water.

Nutrients per Serving

Calories: 371, Calories from Fat: 24%, Total Fat: 10 g, Saturated Fat: 1 g, Protein: 10 g, Carbohydrate: 60 g, Cholesterol: 0 mg, Sodium: 561 mg, Fiber: 5 g

• excellent source of complex carbohydrates

• brown rice provides three times the fiber of white rice, and it is more slowly digested

Creamy Spinach and Brown Rice

- 1½ cups sliced fresh mushrooms
- ½ cup thinly sliced leek, white part only
- 2 teaspoons reduced-calorie margarine
- 2 cups fat-free (skim) milk
- ½ cup brown rice
- ⅓ cup shredded low-fat Swiss cheese
- 1 tablespoon chopped fresh thyme *or* 1 teaspoon dried thyme leaves, crushed
- ⅛ teaspoon black pepper
- 2 cups chopped stemmed washed spinach

Cook and stir mushrooms and leek in margarine in medium saucepan over medium-high heat until leek is tender. Add milk and brown rice. Bring to a boil over medium-high heat. Reduce heat to medium-low. Cover; simmer 45 to 50 minutes or until rice is tender, stirring frequently. Remove from heat.

Add cheese, thyme and pepper. Cook and stir until cheese melts. Stir in spinach. Cover; let stand 5 minutes.

Makes 4 servings

Nutrients per Serving

Calories: 190, Calories from Fat: 19%, Total Fat: 4 g, Saturated Fat: <1 g, Protein: 11 g, Carbohydrate: 29 g, Cholesterol: 8 mg, Sodium: 158 mg, Fiber: 3 g

South-of-the-Border Lunch Express

- ½ cup chopped tomato
- ¼ cup chunky salsa
- ¼ cup drained and rinsed black beans
- ¼ cup frozen whole kernel corn, thawed
- 1 teaspoon chopped fresh cilantro
- ¼ teaspoon bottled chopped garlic
- Dash ground red pepper
- 1 cup cooked brown rice
- Reduced-fat Cheddar cheese (optional)

1. Combine tomato, salsa, beans, corn, cilantro, garlic and pepper in 1-quart microwavable bowl. Cover with vented plastic wrap. Microwave at HIGH 1 to 1½ minutes or until heated through; stir.

2. Microwave rice at HIGH 1 to 1½ minutes in 1-quart microwavable dish or until heated through. Top with tomato mixture and cheese.

Makes 1 serving

Nutrients per Serving

Calories: 345, Calories from Fat: 7%, Total Fat: 3 g, Saturated Fat: <1 g, Protein: 14 g, Carbohydrate: 74 g, Cholesterol: 0 mg, Sodium: 610 mg, Fiber: 11 g

South-of-the-Border Lunch Express

Spinach

Sensational Spinach Salad with Orange Poppyseed Vinaigrette

¼ cup orange juice
3 tablespoons red wine vinegar
2 tablespoons sugar
1 tablespoon olive oil
1 teaspoon grated orange peel
1 teaspoon poppy seeds
¼ teaspoon salt
9 cups washed and torn spinach leaves
1 can (15 ounces) chilled mandarin orange segments, drained
1½ cups fresh sliced mushrooms
1 small red onion, sliced and separated into rings
3 cooked egg whites, coarsely chopped

1. To prepare vinaigrette, combine orange juice, vinegar, sugar, olive oil, orange peel, poppy seeds and salt in small bowl until well blended.

2. To prepare salad, combine spinach, orange segments, mushrooms, onion and egg whites in large serving bowl. Pour vinaigrette over spinach mixture just before serving; toss to coat. Serve immediately. *Makes 6 servings*

Nutrients per Serving

Calories: 112, Calories from Fat: 23%, Total Fat: 3 g, Saturated Fat: <1 g, Protein: 6 g, Carbohydrate: 17 g, Cholesterol: 0 mg, Sodium: 186 mg, Fiber: 3 g

- loaded with vitamins and minerals, some of which are hard to find in other foods
- reasonably high in fiber—twice as much as most other cooking or salad greens
- great source of beta-carotene and vitamin C

Hot and Spicy Spinach

1 red bell pepper, cut into 1-inch pieces
1 clove garlic, minced
1 pound prewashed fresh spinach, rinsed and chopped
1 tablespoon prepared mustard
1 teaspoon lemon juice
¼ teaspoon red pepper flakes

1. Spray large skillet with nonstick cooking spray; heat over medium heat. Add red bell pepper and garlic; cook and stir 3 minutes.

2. Add spinach; cook and stir 3 minutes or just until spinach begins to wilt.

3. Stir in mustard, lemon juice and red pepper flakes. Serve immediately.

Makes 4 servings

Tip: To obtain the maximum nutritional value from spinach, cook it for the shortest possible time. The vitamins in spinach and other greens are soluble in water and fats and are therefore lost during long cooking.

Nutrients per Serving

Calories: 37, Calories from Fat: 12%, Total Fat: 1 g, Saturated Fat: <1 g, Protein: 4 g, Carbohydrate: 6 g, Cholesterol: 0 mg, Sodium: 138 mg, Fiber: 3 g

Middle-Eastern Spinach Salad

¼ cup lemon juice
1 tablespoon olive oil
1 tablespoon packed light brown sugar
½ teaspoon curry powder
1 pound fresh spinach
½ cup golden raisins
¼ cup minced red onion
¼ cup thin red onion slices

For dressing, combine lemon juice, oil, sugar and curry powder in small bowl with wire whisk until blended; set aside.

Wash spinach well to remove sand and grit; remove stems and bruised leaves. Drain well; pat dry with paper towels. Tear spinach into bite-sized pieces.

Toss spinach, raisins, minced onion and onion slices in large bowl. Add dressing; toss gently to coat.

Makes 4 servings

Nutrients per Serving

Calories: 142, Calories from Fat: 22%, Total Fat: 4 g, Saturated Fat: 1 g, Protein: 4 g, Carbohydrate: 27 g, Cholesterol: 0 mg, Sodium: 94 mg, Fiber: 4 g

Hot and Spicy Spinach

Squash

Spaghetti Squash Primavera

2 teaspoons vegetable oil
½ teaspoon finely chopped garlic
¼ cup finely chopped red onion
¼ cup thinly sliced carrot
¼ cup thinly sliced red bell pepper
¼ cup thinly sliced green bell pepper
1 can (14½ ounces) Italian-style stewed tomatoes, undrained
½ cup thinly sliced yellow squash
½ cup thinly sliced zucchini
½ cup frozen whole kernel corn, thawed
½ teaspoon dried oregano leaves
⅛ teaspoon dried thyme leaves
1 spaghetti squash (about 2 pounds)
4 teaspoons grated Parmesan cheese (optional)
2 tablespoons finely chopped fresh parsley

1. Heat oil in large skillet over medium-high heat until hot. Add garlic. Cook and stir 3 minutes. Add onion, carrot and peppers. Cook and stir 3 minutes. Add tomatoes, yellow squash, zucchini, corn, oregano and thyme. Cook 5 minutes or until heated through, stirring occasionally.

2. Cut spaghetti squash lengthwise in half. Remove seeds. Cover with plastic wrap. Microwave at HIGH 9 minutes or until squash separates easily into strands when tested with fork.

3. Cut each squash half lengthwise in half; separate strands with fork. Spoon vegetables evenly over squash. Top servings with cheese and parsley before serving. *Makes 4 servings*

Nutrients per Serving

Calories: 101, Calories from Fat: 25%, Total Fat: 3 g, Saturated Fat: <1 g, Protein: 3 g, Carbohydrate: 18 g, Cholesterol: 0 mg, Sodium: 11 mg, Fiber: 5 g

• low in calories, high in fiber and easily digested

• winter varieties are chockful of beta-carotene, which can help protect the lungs from diseases

Baked Acorn Squash with Apples and Raisins

2 medium acorn squash (about 2¼ pounds)
⅓ cup reduced-calorie pancake syrup
1 Granny Smith apple, peeled, cored, coarsely chopped
¼ cup seedless raisins
⅛ teaspoon ground nutmeg
1½ teaspoons cornstarch
2 tablespoons water

Preheat oven to 400°F. Cut squash into halves; remove seeds. Place squash, cut sides down, in 13×9-inch baking dish. Add 1 cup water; bake 40 minutes or until fork-tender. Turn squash cut sides up.

Meanwhile, heat syrup in medium saucepan over medium heat. Add apple, raisins and nutmeg; cook and stir about 8 minutes. Blend cornstarch and 2 tablespoons water; stir into saucepan. Cook and stir over medium-high heat until mixture boils and thickens. Cook and stir 2 minutes more. Divide mixture among squash halves. Return squash to oven; bake 10 minutes more or until heated through.

Makes 4 servings

Nutrients per Serving

Calories: 196, Calories from Fat: 1%, Total Fat: <1 g, Saturated Fat: <1 g, Protein: 2 g, Carbohydrate: 52 g, Cholesterol: 0 mg, Sodium: 152 mg, Fiber: 6 g

Orzo and Summer Squash Salad

1⅓ cups (8 ounces) orzo pasta, uncooked
3 cups diced zucchini and/or yellow summer squash (½-inch pieces)
1 cup diced tomato
½ cup prepared light Caesar salad dressing
1 teaspoon dried basil leaves
Fresh spinach leaves
Salt and black pepper

1. Cook orzo according to package directions for 7 minutes. Add squash to orzo; return to a boil. Cook 1 to 2 minutes more or until orzo and squash are tender. Drain well; rinse under cold water to stop cooking.

2. Place mixture in large bowl; stir in tomato. Pour dressing over salad; sprinkle with basil. Toss gently to coat. Cover and refrigerate until cool. Serve salad over spinach leaves. Season to taste with salt and pepper.

Makes 6 (1-cup) servings

Nutrients per Serving

Calories: 184, Calories from Fat: 11%, Total Fat: 2 g, Saturated Fat: <1 g, Protein: 6 g, Carbohydrate: 35 g, Cholesterol: 7 mg, Sodium: 133 mg, Fiber: 3 g

Orzo and Summer Squash Salad

SQUASH
SQUASH

Sweet Potatoes

Curried Creamy Sweet Potato Soup

4 cups water
1 pound sweet potatoes, peeled and cut into 1-inch cubes
1 tablespoon plus 1 teaspoon butter or margarine, divided
2 cups finely chopped yellow onions
2 cups fat-free (skim) milk, divided
¾ teaspoon curry powder
½ teaspoon salt
Dash ground red pepper (optional)

Bring water to a boil in large saucepan over high heat. Add potatoes; return to a boil. Reduce heat to medium-low and simmer, uncovered, 15 minutes or until potatoes are tender.

Meanwhile, heat medium nonstick skillet over medium-high heat until hot. Coat with nonstick cooking spray; add 1 teaspoon butter and tilt skillet to coat bottom. Add onions; cook 8 minutes or until tender and golden.

Drain potatoes; place in blender with onions, 1 cup milk, curry powder, salt and ground red pepper. Blend until completely smooth. Return potato mixture to saucepan and stir in remaining 1 cup milk. Cook 5 minutes over medium-high heat or until heated through. Remove from heat and stir in remaining 1 tablespoon butter.

Makes 3 cups
(¾ cup per appetizer serving)

Nutrients per Serving

Calories: 201, Calories from Fat: 20%, Total Fat: 5 g, Saturated Fat: 3 g, Protein: 7 g, Carbohydrate: 35 g, Cholesterol: 13 mg, Sodium: 406 mg, Fiber: 4 g

- a nutrient-dense, high-fiber food that's fat free
- provides as much beta-carotene as a serving of carrots
- rich in potassium and vitamin C

Tofu

- one of the best plant sources of protein, lighter and easier to digest than poultry or beef
- provides a reasonable amount of iron
- a good source of the B vitamins, which can help prevent nervous disorders and digestive distress
- soybeans contain at least five known anticancer agents

Quick Fruited Couscous

2¼ cups orange juice
1 tablespoon margarine
1 teaspoon grated orange peel
½ teaspoon salt
1 package (10 ounces) couscous
1 medium orange, peeled, separated into sections and cut into halves
1 cup red grapes, cut into halves
6 ounces firm tofu, drained and cubed
½ cup golden raisins

1. Bring orange juice, margarine, orange peel and salt to a boil in large saucepan over high heat. Stir in couscous; cover and remove from heat. Let stand 5 minutes.

2. Fluff couscous with fork; stir in orange pieces, grapes, tofu and raisins until well blended. Serve immediately or cover and refrigerate.

Makes 8 servings

Nutrients per Serving

Calories: 247, Calories from Fat: 11%, Total Fat: 3 g, Saturated Fat: 1 g, Protein: 7 g, Carbohydrate: 49 g, Cholesterol: 0 mg, Sodium: 157 mg, Fiber: 7 g

Spinach and Tomato Tofu Toss

Nonstick cooking spray
¾ cup chopped onion
1 teaspoon chopped garlic
1 package (10 ounces) extra-firm tofu, drained and cut into ½-inch cubes
2 teaspoons soy sauce
¼ teaspoon ground black pepper
¼ pound washed spinach leaves, divided
4 whole wheat pitas, cut in half
2 large ripe tomatoes, chopped
¾ cup chopped red bell pepper

1. Spray large nonstick skillet with cooking spray; heat over medium heat until hot. Add onion and garlic. Cook and stir 2 minutes. Add tofu, soy sauce and black pepper to skillet; toss until well combined. Cook over medium heat 3 to 4 minutes or until heated through. Remove from heat and cool slightly.

2. Set aside 8 whole spinach leaves; tear remaining leaves into bite-size pieces. Line pita halves with whole spinach leaves. Add tomatoes, torn spinach and bell peppers to tofu mixture; toss to combine. Fill pita halves with tofu mixture. Serve immediately. *Makes 4 servings*

Nutrients per Serving

Calories: 324, Calories from Fat: 21%, Total Fat: 8 g, Saturated Fat: 1 g, Protein: 20 g, Carbohydrate: 49 g, Cholesterol: 0 mg, Sodium: 561 mg, Fiber: 4 g

Tofu Stir-Fry

2 cups uncooked instant rice
2 teaspoons vegetable oil
2 cups broccoli florets
1 large carrot, sliced
½ green bell pepper, sliced
¼ cup frozen chopped onion
½ cup teriyaki sauce
½ cup orange juice
1 tablespoon cornstarch
1 teaspoon bottled minced garlic
½ teaspoon ground ginger
¼ to ½ teaspoon hot pepper sauce
1 package (10½ ounces) reduced-fat firm tofu, drained and cubed

1. Cook rice according to package directions.

2. While rice is cooking, heat oil in large skillet. Add broccoli, carrot, bell pepper and onion; cook and stir 3 minutes.

3. Combine teriyaki sauce, orange juice, cornstarch, garlic, ginger and pepper sauce in small bowl; mix well. Pour sauce over vegetables in skillet. Bring to a boil; cook and stir 1 minute.

4. Add tofu to skillet; stir gently to coat with sauce. Serve over rice. Garnish, if desired. *Makes 4 servings*

Nutrients per Serving

Calories: 320, Calories from Fat: 11%, Total Fat: 4 g, Protein: 13 g, Carbohydrate: 60 g, Cholesterol: 0 mg, Sodium: 1472 mg, Fiber: 4 g

Bean Threads with Tofu and Vegetables

- 8 ounces firm tofu, drained and cubed
- 1 tablespoon dark sesame oil
- 3 teaspoons low-sodium soy sauce, divided
- 1 can (about 14 ounces) fat-free, low-sodium chicken broth
- 1 package (3¾ ounces) bean threads
- 1 package (16 ounces) frozen mixed vegetable medley such as broccoli, carrots and red pepper, thawed
- ¼ cup rice wine vinegar
- ½ teaspoon red pepper flakes

1. Place tofu on shallow plate; drizzle with oil and 1½ teaspoons soy sauce.

2. Combine broth and remaining 1½ teaspoons soy sauce in deep skillet or large saucepan. Bring to a boil over high heat; reduce heat. Add bean threads; simmer, uncovered, 7 minutes or until noodles absorb liquid, stirring occasionally to separate noodles.

3. Stir in vegetables and vinegar; heat through. Stir in tofu mixture and red pepper flakes; heat about 1 minute.

Makes 6 side-dish servings

Nutrients per Serving

Calories: 167, Calories from Fat: 30%, Total Fat: 6 g, Saturated Fat: 1 g, Protein: 8 g, Carbohydrate: 23 g, Cholesterol: 0 mg, Sodium: 130 mg, Fiber: 3 g

Tofu is made from soybeans that have been soaked, mashed, cooked and filtered to produce soy milk. The milk is then curdled, and the curds that form are drained and pressed into blocks as the whey drains off.

Tomatoes

Roasted Red Pepper & Tomato Casserole

1 jar (12 ounces) roasted red peppers, drained
1½ teaspoons red wine vinegar
1 teaspoon olive oil
1 clove garlic, minced
¼ teaspoon salt
¼ teaspoon black pepper
⅓ cup grated Parmesan cheese, divided
3 medium tomatoes (about 1½ pounds), sliced
½ cup (about 1 ounce) herb-flavored croutons, crushed

1. Combine red peppers, vinegar, oil, garlic, salt and black pepper in food processor; process using on/off pulsing action 1 minute until slightly chunky. Reserve 2 tablespoons cheese for garnish. Stir remaining cheese into red pepper mixture.

2. Arrange tomato slices in 8-inch round microwavable baking dish; microwave at HIGH 1 minute. Spoon red pepper mixture on top; microwave at HIGH 2 to 3 minutes or until tomatoes are slightly soft.

3. Sprinkle with reserved cheese and croutons.

Makes 6 servings

Nutrients per Serving

Calories: 80, Calories from Fat: 30%, Total Fat: 2 g, Saturated Fat: 1 g, Protein: 3 g, Carbohydrate: 9 g, Cholesterol: 3 mg, Sodium: 342 mg, Fiber: 1 g

- rich in vitamin C, which helps maintain a healthy immune system
- new research finds tomatoes prominent in the diets of people less prone to cancer
- offer a good dose of beta-carotene and potassium

Yogurt

- a complete protein source
- provides bone-building calcium in a form more easily digested than calcium from milk
- provides riboflavin, vitamin B12 and many minerals
- research suggests that eating yogurt regularly helps boost the immune function, warding off colds and possibly cancer

Triple Berry Breakfast Parfait

2 cups vanilla sugar-free nonfat yogurt
¼ teaspoon ground cinnamon
1 cup sliced strawberries
½ cup blueberries
½ cup raspberries
1 cup low-fat granola without raisins

1. Combine yogurt and cinnamon in small bowl. Combine strawberries, blueberries and raspberries in medium bowl.

2. For each parfait, layer ¼ cup fruit mixture, 2 tablespoons granola and ¼ cup yogurt mixture in parfait glass. Repeat layers. Garnish with mint leaves, if desired.

Makes 4 servings

Nutrients per Serving

Calories: 236, Calories from Fat: 9%, Total Fat: 2 g, Saturated Fat: <1 g, Protein: 9 g, Carbohydrate: 49 g, Cholesterol: 0 mg, Sodium: 101 mg, Fiber: 2 g

Fresh Fruits with Cranberry Yogurt Sauce

6 cups baby greens
3 slices fresh pineapple, peeled and halved
2 kiwifruit
1 banana
½ cantaloupe
1 medium orange
1 medium apple
1 cup cranberries
¼ cup sugar
1½ cups vanilla low fat yogurt

1. Divide baby greens and pineapple evenly among salad plates. Peel and thinly slice kiwifruit and banana; add to salad plates. Remove rind from cantaloupe; slice cantaloupe and add to other fruits.

2. Using a vegetable peeler, remove peel from orange. Cut peel into 1-inch sections and place in food processor or blender. Cut peeled orange into quarters and place in food processor or blender. Peel, core and slice apple. Add cranberries, apple and sugar to food processor or blender; process 10 seconds or until finely chopped, scraping side of bowl as needed. Add yogurt; process until blended. Pour sauce over fruits and greens. Serve immediately. *Makes 6 servings*

Nutrients per Serving

Calories: 200, Calories from Fat: 6%, Total Fat: 1 g, Saturated Fat: <1 g, Protein: 5 g, Carbohydrate: 46 g, Cholesterol: 3 mg, Sodium: 91 mg, Fiber: 6 g

Strawberries with Honeyed Yogurt Sauce

1 quart fresh strawberries
1 cup plain low-fat yogurt
1 tablespoon orange juice
1 to 2 teaspoons honey
Ground cinnamon

Rinse and hull strawberries. Combine yogurt, juice, honey and cinnamon to taste in small bowl; mix well. Serve sauce over berries.

Makes 4 servings

Nutrients per Serving

Calories: 88, Calories from Fat: 14%, Total Fat: 1 g, Saturated Fat: 1 g, Protein: 4 g, Carbohydrate: 16 g, Cholesterol: 4 mg, Sodium: 41 mg, Fiber: 4 g

Index